Amazing Animals
COLOR BY NUMBERS

David Woodroffe

SIRIUS

SIRIUS

This edition published in 2024 by Sirius Publishing, a division of
Arcturus Publishing Limited,
26/27 Bickels Yard, 151–153 Bermondsey Street,
London SE1 3HA

ISBN: 978-1-3988-4046-1
CH011885NT
Supplier 29, Date 0424, PI 00005891

Printed in China

INTRODUCTION

Have you ever wanted to stalk with leopards, gallop with ponies, or swim with sharks? Dive in to this exciting color-by-number collection of our planet's diverse array of animals, from sly chameleons to high-flying eagles. This collection will allow you to journey across the animal kingdom, as you create artworks of both the tiniest and mightiest of species.

Each image is numbered so that, by referring to the color key printed on the inside back cover, you can give life to these fantastic creatures. Choose your animal, whether it be a mammal, an amphibian, reptile, bird, fish, or insect. If there is no number that means the space should be left white or colored with a white pencil. Take comfort in knowing that by simply following the guided numbers, you can render a stunningly accurate portrait of your animal at its best.

While the more complex scenes will require more time and patience, it will be hugely rewarding to see your chosen animal thriving in its natural habitat.

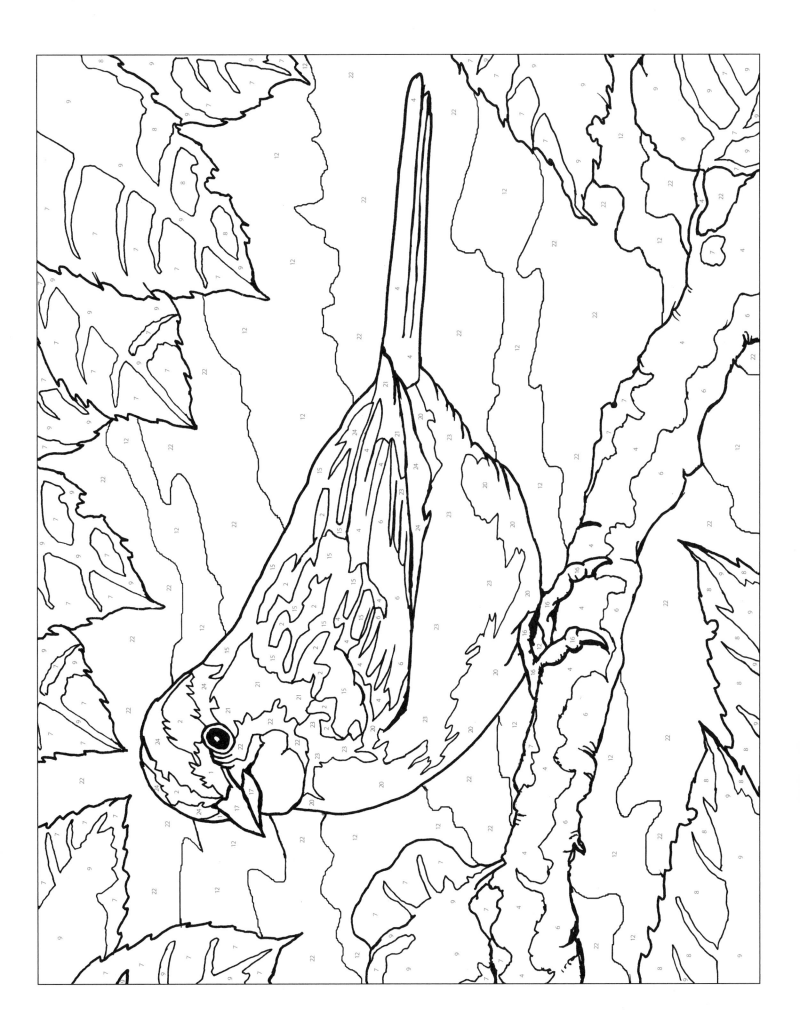

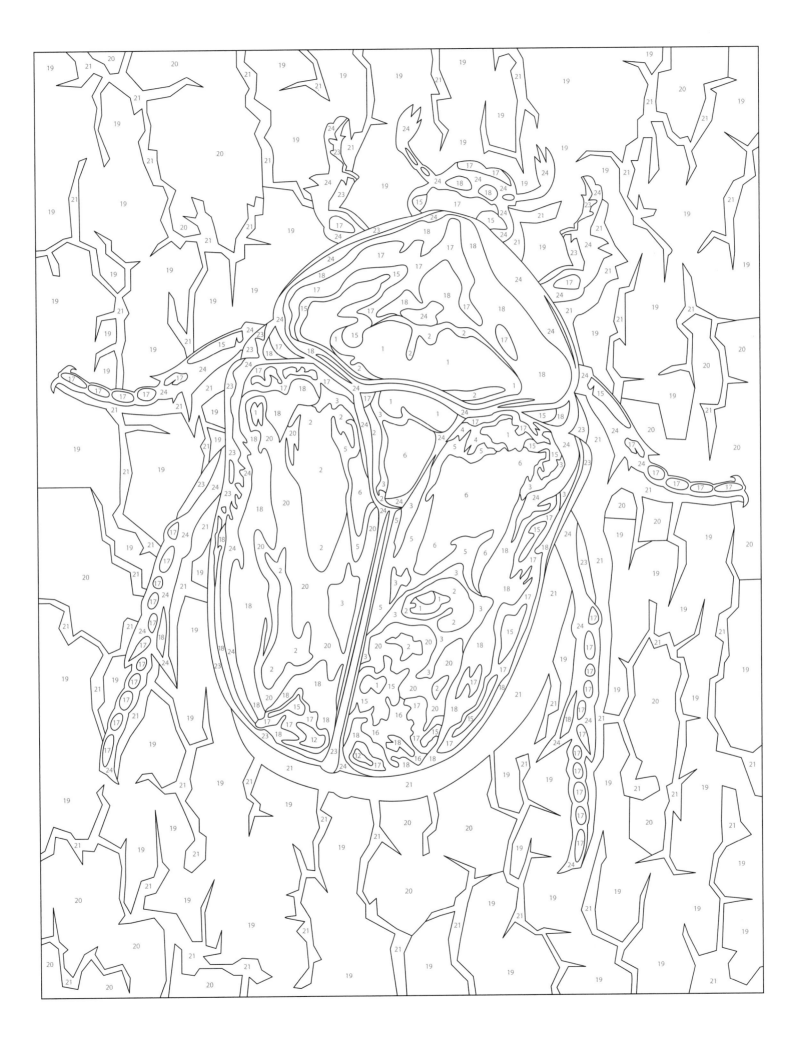